# REMBRANDT COLORING BOOK

---

## 8 MASTERPIECES FROM THE MASTER

---

ARTHUR BENJAMIN

# ABOUT THE BOOK

Rembrandt was one of the greatest artists of his time; his name wields power and respect today, all undoubtedly homage to the great artistry of his work. Discover some of Rembrandt's greatest masterpieces through a this gorgeously illustrated collection of Rembrandt's paintings formatted specifically for coloring.

# CONTENTS

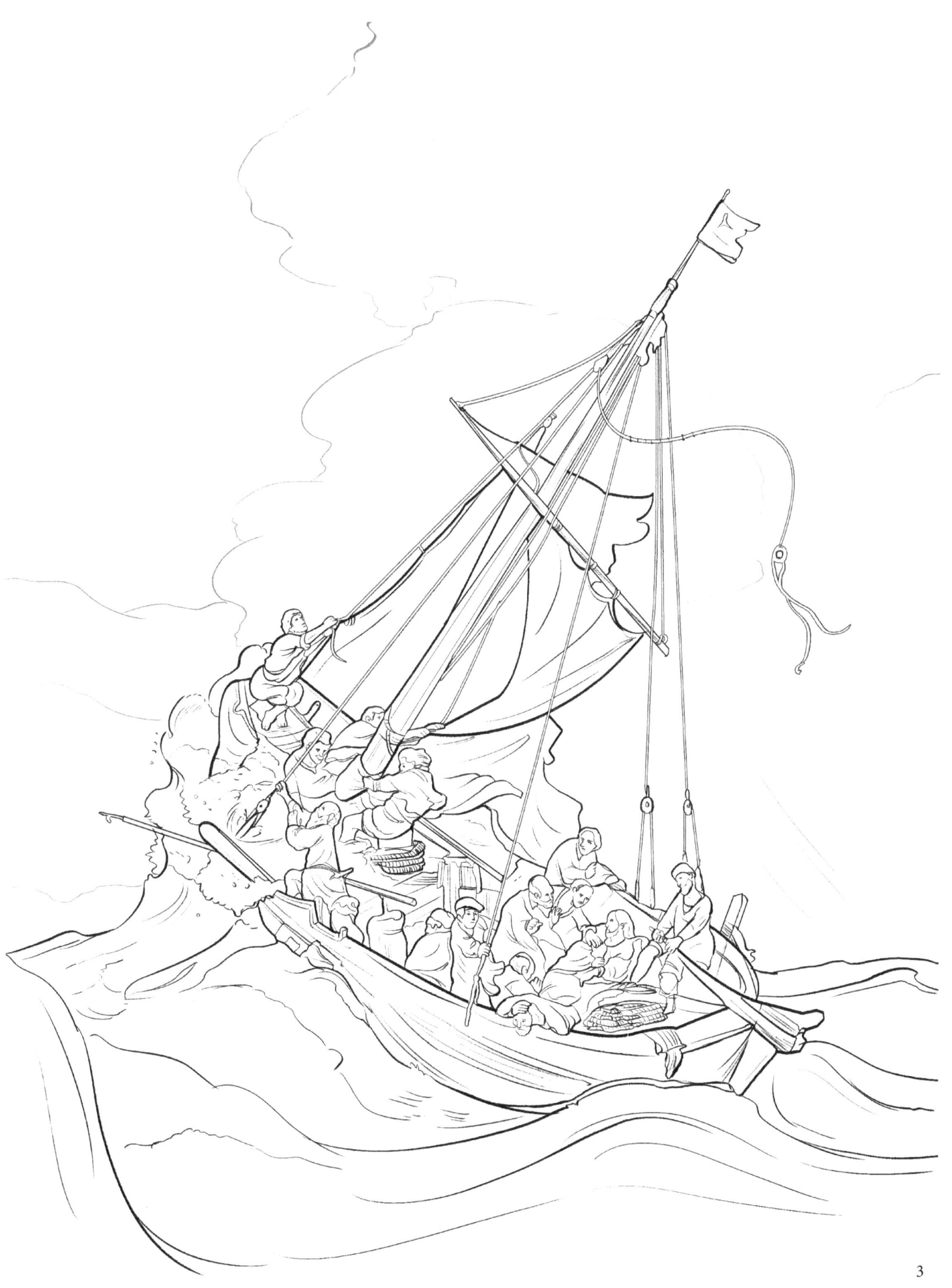

**Plate 1.**

*Christ in the Storm on the Sea of Galilee, 1633, missing
(stolen in 1990 from Isabella Stewart Gardner Museum, Boston).*

*Rembrandt painted landscapes and waterscapes mainly as parts of narrative scenes. Here is a marine painting with a Bible story. Terrified and doubtful, Christ's companions wake him. Their fishing boat is caught in a storm, but Christ remains calm and stops the tempest. This is a comforting moral lesson about lack of faith and a metaphor of wisdom and salvation. At the same time, it is a fine example of maritime art. For Rembrandt, seascape is the picture of men at sea, so he made a striking composition, with intense motion, confident drawing and polished brushwork.*

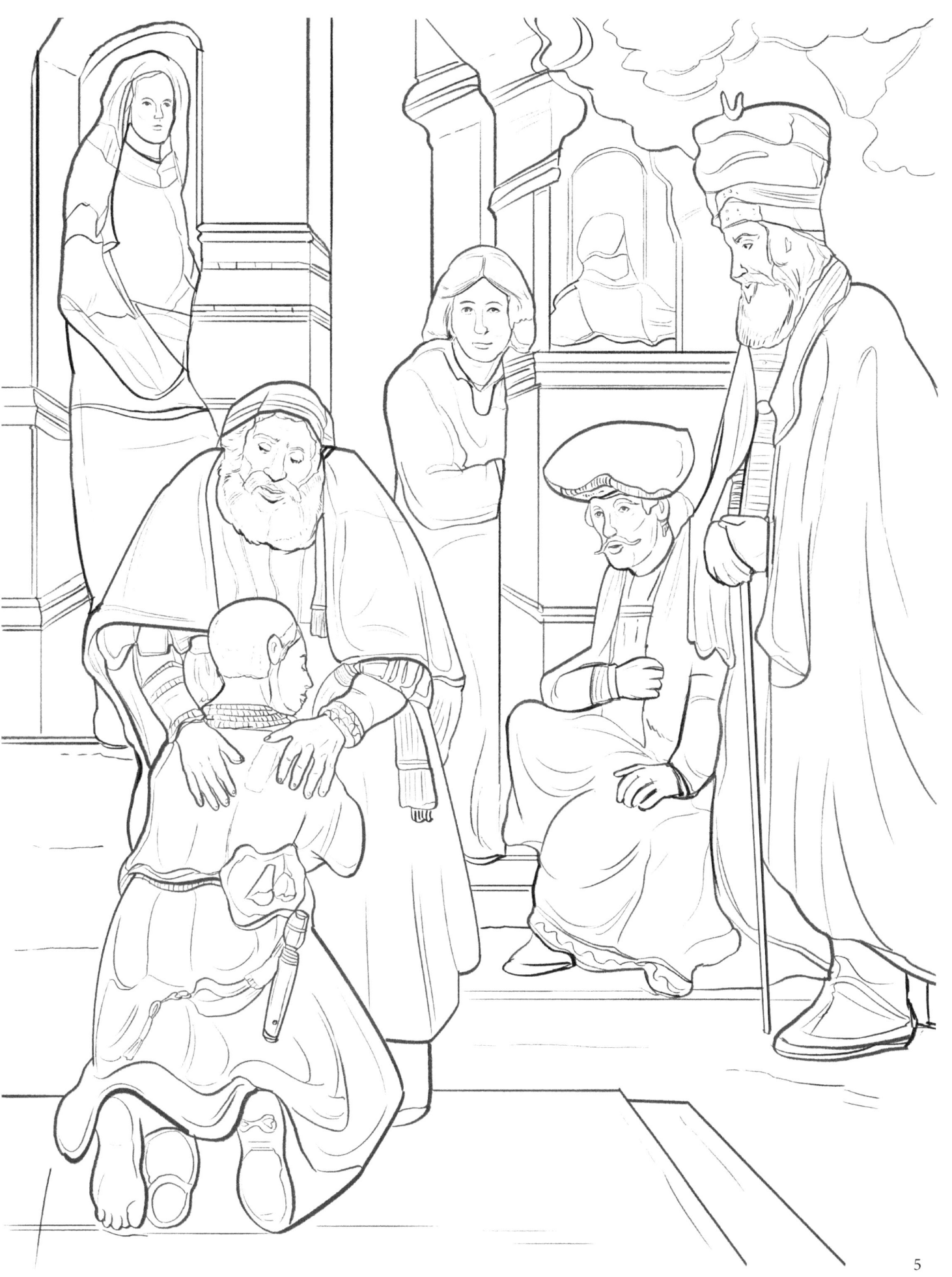

**Plate 2.**

*The Abduction of Europa, 1632, J. Paul Getty Museum, Los Angeles.*

*Inspired by Ovid's Metamorphoses, Rembrandt depicted this mythological scene as a history painting with the landscape. Jupiter (Zeus), in the form of a white bull, carries away Phoenician princess Europa over the sea, towards the Island of Crete. Theatrical gestures of her entourage and contrast of light and shadow underline the dramatic moment. Golden details on the carriage and the women's garment suggest precision of the author's observation and his virtuosity. Rembrandt's early style is descriptive, and the imaginative landscape, combined with a view of a contemporary city, introduces his interest in light effects.*

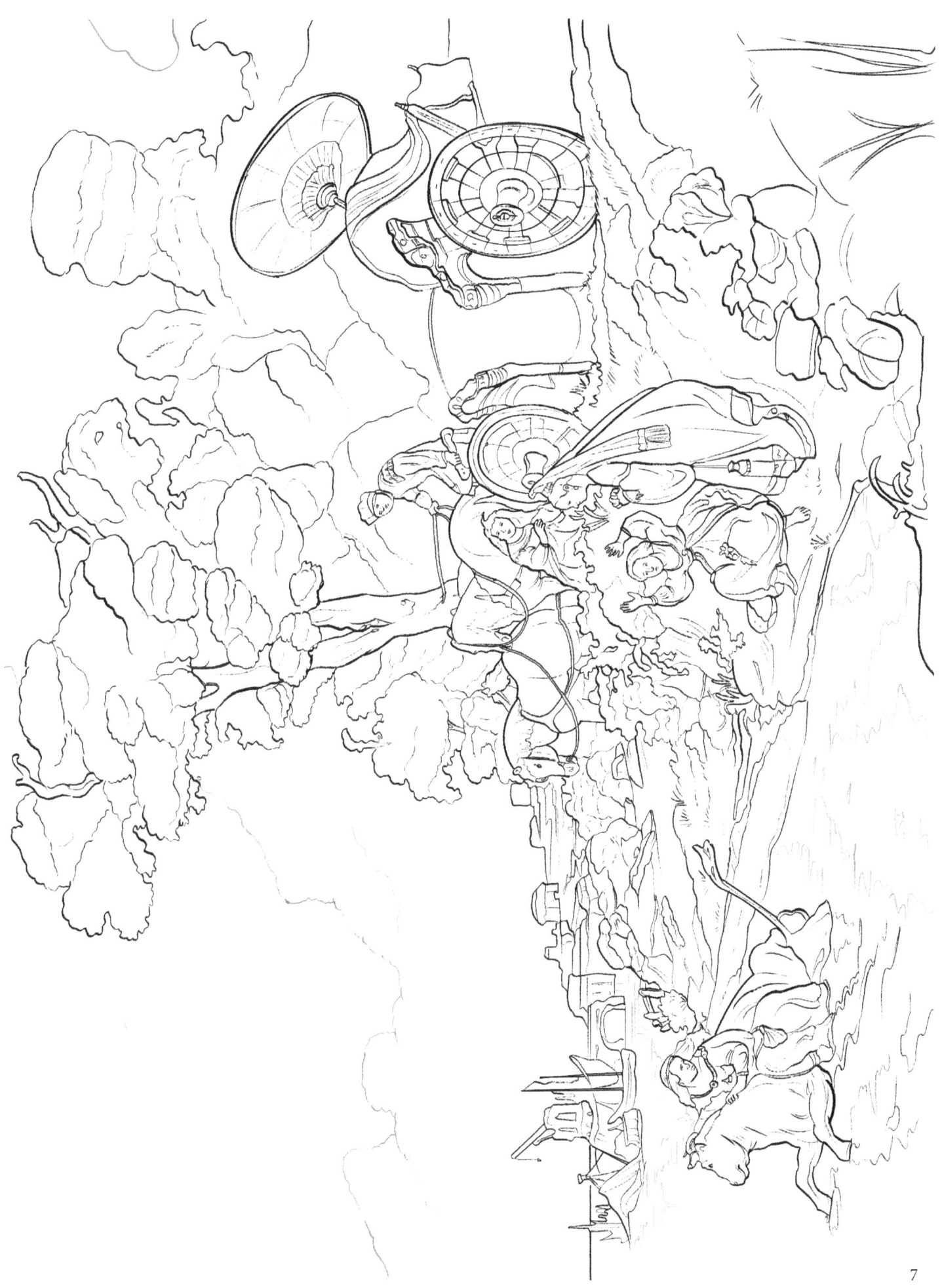

**Plate 3.**

*The Return of the Prodigal Son, c. 1668, State Hermitage Museum, Saint Petersburg.*

*This large, serene picture tells the parable of the prodigal son from the Gospel of Luke. The painter illustrated the emotional reunion of father and son, in the presence of the mother, brother and two silent witnesses. The son lost his fortune, so he comes back to his father's home. As God forgives those who repent, the family embraces the remorseful, destitute man, in this sacred moment of love and mercy. Rembrandt's late style shows innovative, quick and spontaneous brushstrokes. He integrates these improvisations with a realistic approach, and he uses simple décor, a strong contrast between light and darkness and voluminous bodies to present this moving allegory.*

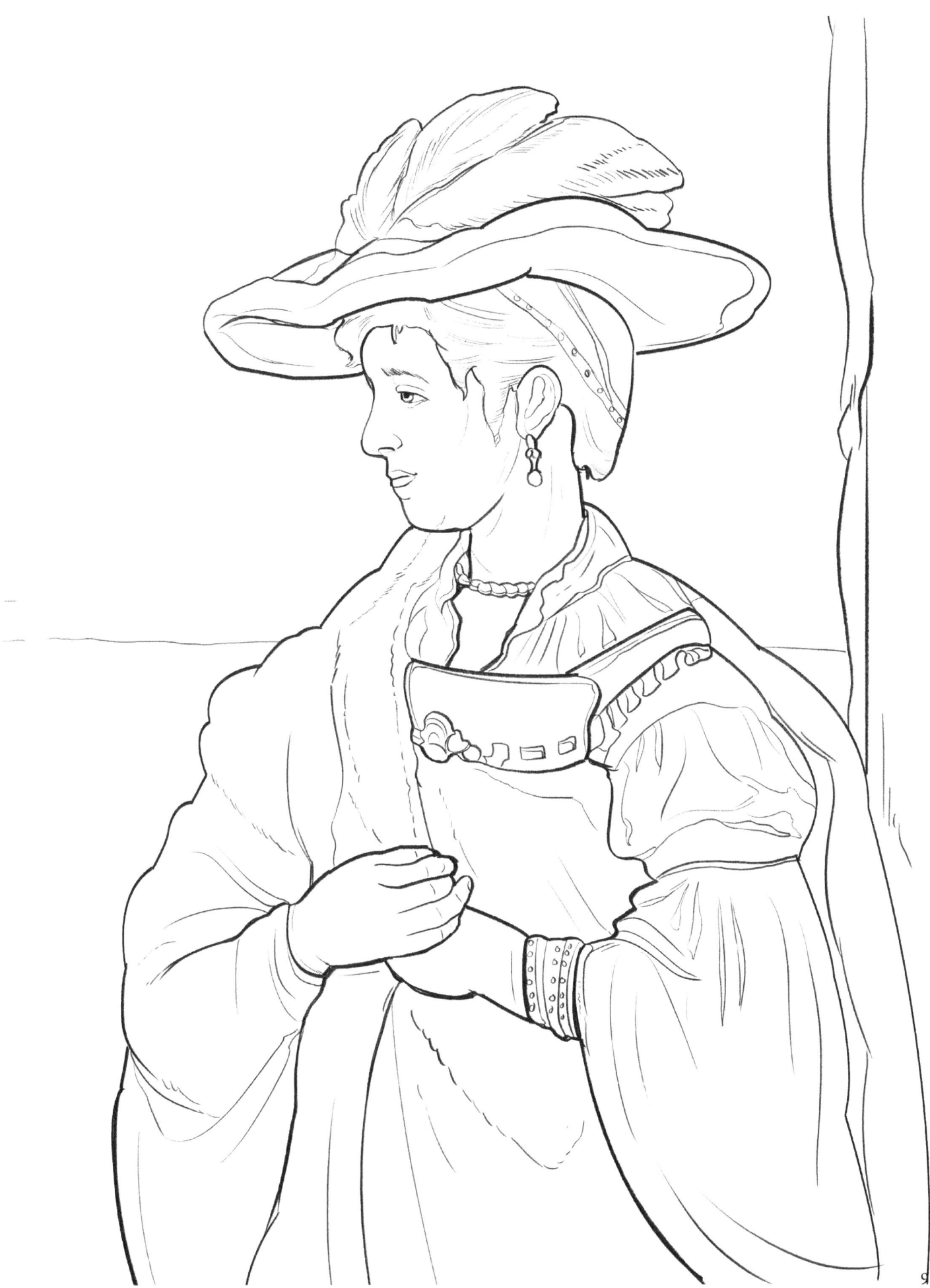

**Plate 4.**

*Saskia van Uylenburgh (in a Red Hat), the Wife of Rembrandt the Painter, Carel Fabritius, the 1640s, Royal Museum of Fine Arts, Antwerp.*

*Carel Fabritius was one of Rembrandt's pupils between 1641 and 1643. He worked mainly in Delft, but few of his paintings survived. This one was made after Rembrandt's portrait of Saskia from 1642 (called Saskia van Uylenburgh in Profile, in Rich Costume, Gemaldegalerie Alte Meister, Kassel). Maestro painted it for his private collection, probably to commemorate his wedding. The couple married in 1634, and Saskia brought good connections and a valuable dowry to her husband. She was Rembrandt's model numerous times, but here she is painted in profile, which is unusual for Rembrandt. She wears a rich, fashionable costume with golden details. Portrait of painter's wife was a popular motif, as a symbol of ideal beauty and social status. In this replica, Fabritius demonstrates his sophisticated technique and captures feminine sensuality.*

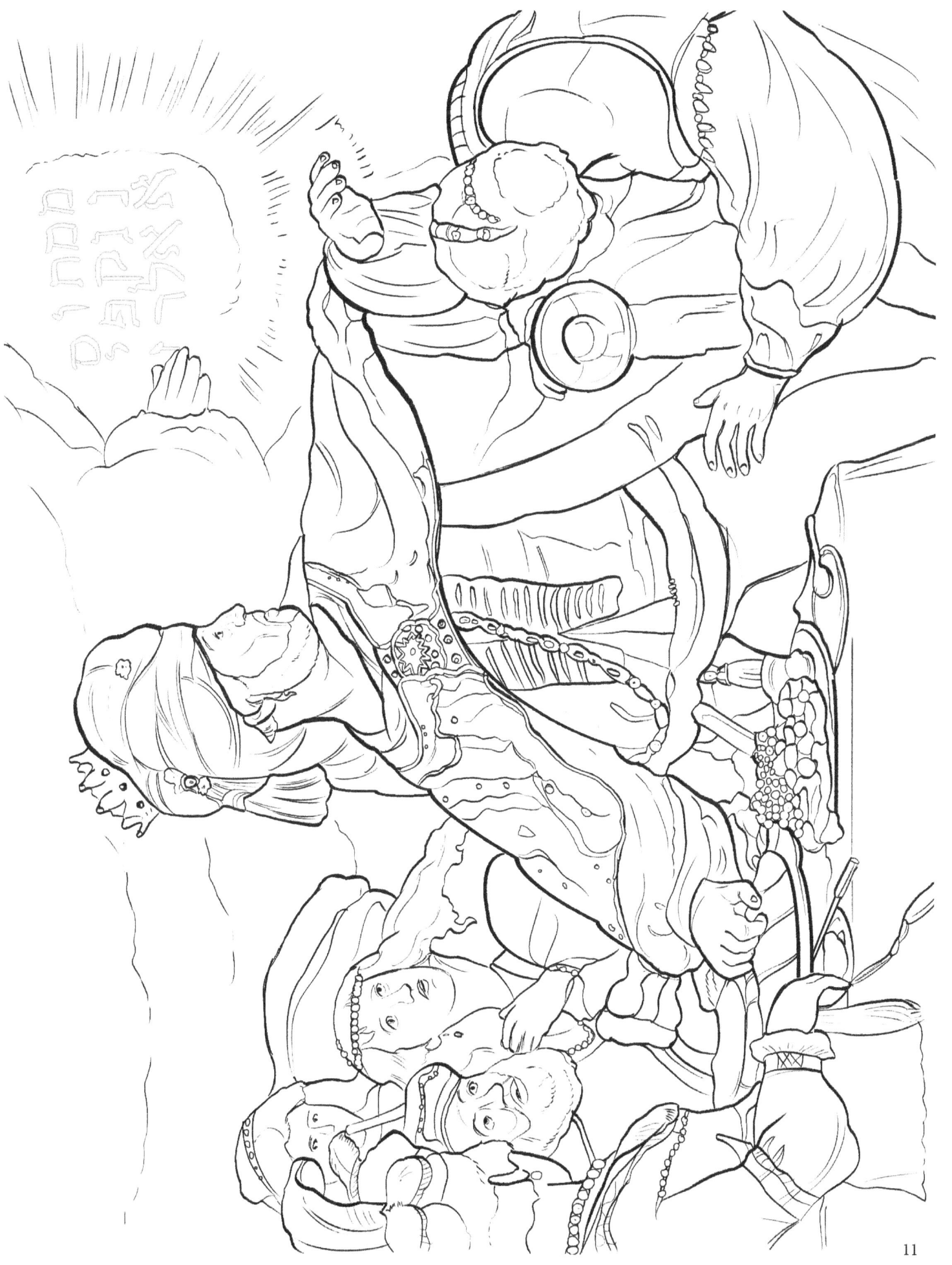

11

**Plate 5.**

*Belshazzar's Feast, 1636-8, National Gallery, London.*

*The Book of Daniel describes the feast of Nebuchadnezzar's son, Belshazzar, the last king of Babylon. During this extravagant banquet, he praised pagan idols and desecrated objects from Solomon's Temple in Jerusalem. Rembrandt paints the turning point of the evening when the divine hand miraculously appeared and wrote the ominous words on the wall. Daniel the Prophet was the only one able to interpret God's message, and the king died that very night. This painting reveals Rembrandt's mature Baroque style. He creates a dynamic composition, with bright light and authentic facial expressions and movements of the protagonists. His intention was to paint accurately and persuasively, so he often consulted eminent rabbi Menasseh ben Israel about Old Testament themes. He was also a passionate collector of curiosities and luxurious artifacts from the Middle East, and he regularly used them as inspiration.*

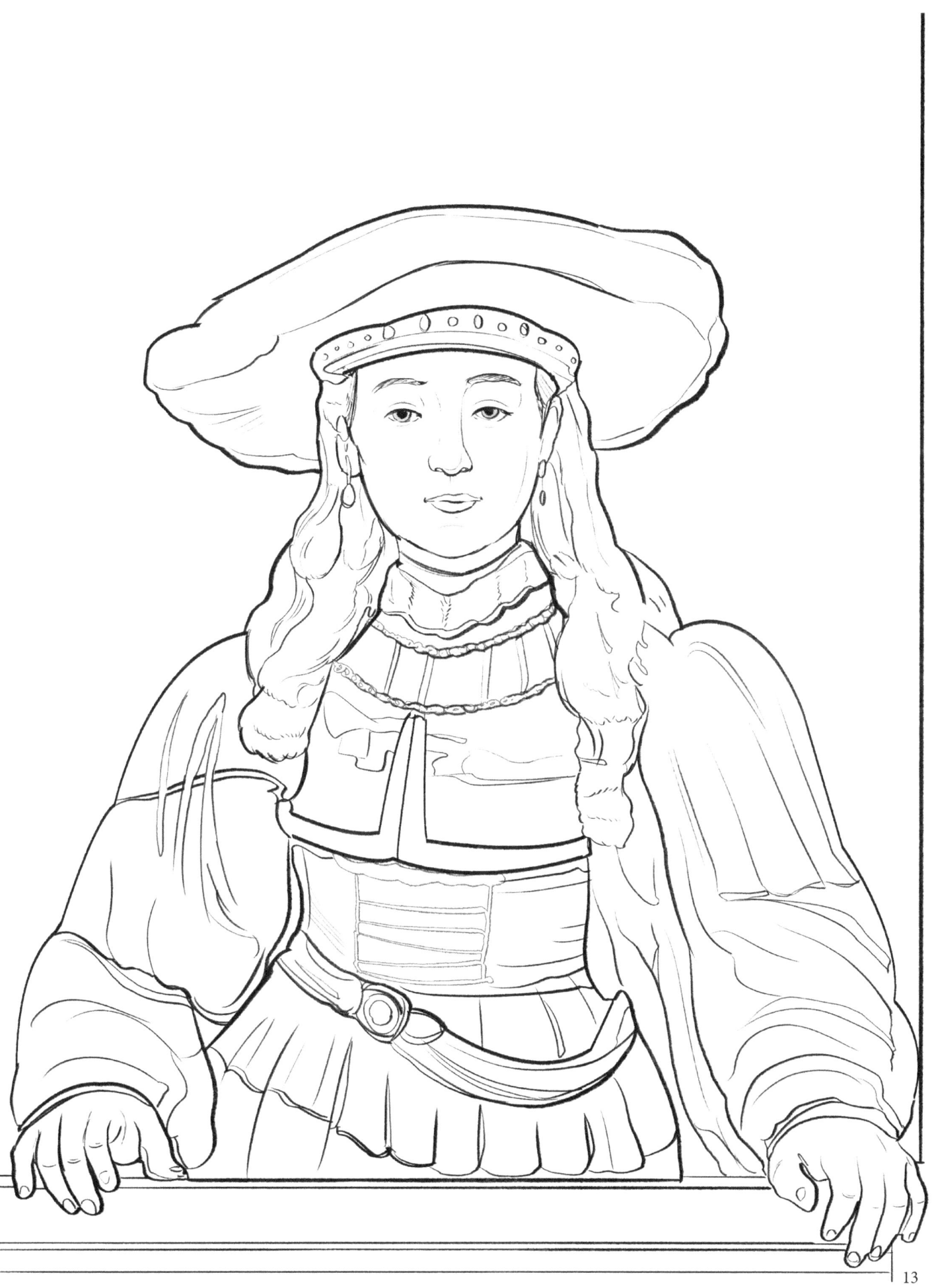

**Plate 6.**

*Girl in a Picture Frame, 1641, Royal Castle, Warsaw.*

*This is an exceptional toning of an unknown, intriguing young woman in a historical costume. Her idealized face and ambiguous personality indicate brevity of life and beauty. The author uses balanced colors and refined texture on a shallow background, but he is the master of illusionism! He plays with light and the picture frame and allows the sitter to come into the space of the viewers. This painting is often mentioned as The Jewish Bride, linked with another artwork from the same collection, called The Father of Jewish Bride, or Scholar at His Writing Table. Rembrandt was close to the Sephardic Jewish community of Amsterdam, and he often painted careful studies of Jewish models.*

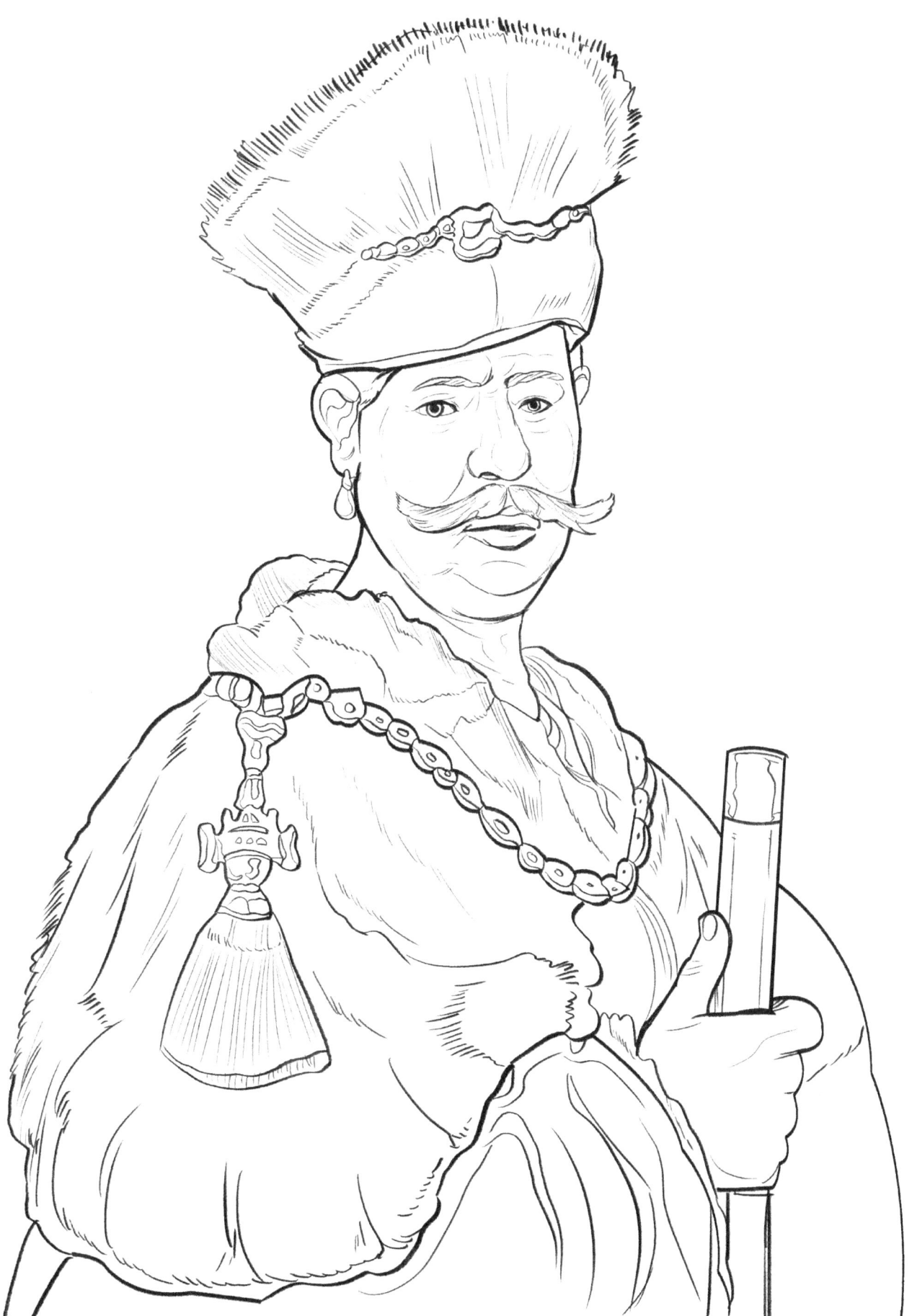

**Plate 7.**

*A Polish Nobleman, 1637, National Gallery of Art, Washington D.C.*

*Rembrandt was the leading portraitist of his time, but this painting is an analysis of face and character type. This is an imaginary Slavic model in exotic clothes. The painter, inspired by brave Polish wars against the Ottoman Empire, wanted to draw a patrician from Eastern Europe. A sincere look towards the spectator, a thick mustache and meticulously painted fur and jewelry confirm Rembrandt's artistic skills. He managed to express integrity of an elderly man, with warm, vibrant colors, a solid figure and exquisite details.*

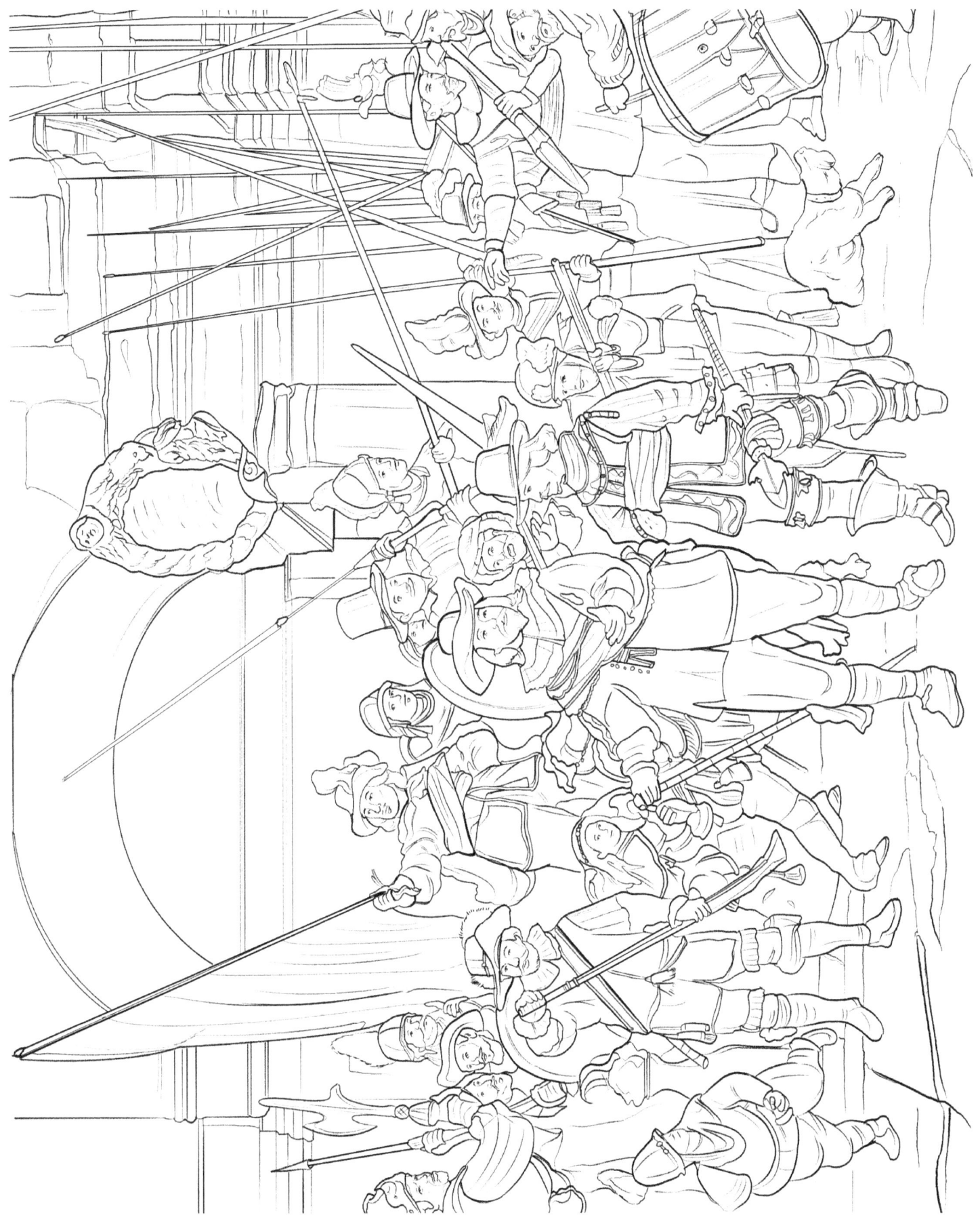

Plate 8.

*The Night Watch, 1642, Rijksmuseum, Amsterdam.*

Group portrait of Amsterdam's militia company was commissioned from Rembrandt in 1639. He designed it as a busy outdoors scene in dark tonality. The guardsmen are in movement, assembling in front of a city gate. Captain Frans Banninck Cocq and Lieutenant Willem van Ruytenburch, illuminated by metaphysical light, lead sixteen militiamen. These figures are not arranged in a traditional manner, and the painting is significantly different than comparable portraits of civic organizations. Rembrandt added more characters and used deep shadows to create a powerful composition. He wanted to emphasize the importance of the company, as a symbol of the city's history, peace and welfare.

# ABOUT THE BOOK

Rembrandt was one of the greatest artists of his time; his name wields power and respect today, all undoubtedly homage to the great artistry of his work. Discover some of Rembrandt's greatest masterpieces through a this gorgeously illustrated collection of Rembrandt's paintings formatted specifically for coloring.